The
Toytown helicopter

Story by Jenny Giles
Illustrations by Richard Hoit

Here is the Toytown Garage.

3

The rain is coming down.

The bus is coming home
to the garage.

The tow truck

and the fire engine

are coming home, too.

"Look at the rain!"

said the tow truck.

"Where is the helicopter?"

"Look at the rain!"

said the bus.

"The helicopter can not

fly home in the rain,"

said the fire engine.

"I am going to look

for the helicopter,"

said the tow truck.

13

"Oh, look!"

said the tow truck.

"The rain is going away.

Here comes the sun."

15

Rrrrr! Rrrrr! Rrrrr!

The Toytown helicopter

is coming home.